NEW YORK KNICKS

By Molly Martin

❦ Creative Education

Up and over: Big Dave DeBusschere shows Knick-size hustle as he collars the ball from Sidney Wicks of the Trail Blazers in 1973 action.

Library of Congress Catalog Card Number: 83-73304

ISBN: 0-87191-984-2

NEW YORK KNICKS

THE LEGACY: The Basketball Association of America started in 1946 with 11 teams. Ony two remain. But those two represent the sport as well as any teams could: the Boston Celtics and the New York Knicks.

MEET THE KNICKS

Some sports teams are tailor-made for their cities.

Take Dallas, Texas for example. Early settlers had to be big and tough to turn the vast Texas plains into big-time cattle country. Today it's not surprising that in Dallas, football's Cowboys are king.

Up in Montreal, Canada things are a little different. There, people just naturally learn the fine art of ice hockey. In Montreal, the National Hockey League's Canadiens are the team to watch.

Now, let's talk about New York City. Oh, sure, the Big Apple has big-league sports of all kinds: football's Jets and Giants, baseball's Mets and Yankees, hockey's Rangers and Islanders, and even Soccer's Cosmos. But if you gaze out at the streets and playgrounds of New York, one sport stands out above the rest. It's basketball.

Yes, the game of basketball is just like the city itself. Smooth, slick, always on the go. Plus, it's easy for a city kid to find a place to play. All you need is a ball and hoop. The rest is up to you.

Whatever the reasons, basketball is THE sport for New Yorkers. And who's at the top of New York's basketball list? The New York Knickerbockers.

Most popular fella: In 1964 it was the Knicks' Tom Gola who won the CYO's annual Most Popular New York Knickerbocker award.

WHO ELSE? March 2, 1962 is an important date in New York Knicks history. That day, against Philadelphia, three different New York players — Richie Guerin, Willie Naulls and Cleveland Buckner — scored more than 30 points each. But that wasn't the most eye-catching part of that game. Philadelphia's center, Wilt Chamberlain scored 100 (yes, one hundred!) points. That was the season "The Stilt" averaged 50.4 points per game. That record may go untouched in the NBA books.

To the people of New York, the Knicks are more than just another National Basketball Association team. They're a first-class club in a first-class city. They're great coaches, such as Joe Lapchick and Red Holzman. Twice the Knicks have won the NBA title. Four more times they've played in the championship series.

But most of all, the Knicks are the more than 200 players who have proudly worn the team's red, white and blue uniforms.

Guys like Carl Braun, Harry Gallatin, Richie Guerin and Willie Naulls in the club's early years.

Or, the Knicks superstars of the late 1960s and early 1970s: Willis Reed, Walt Frazier, Dave DeBusschere, Bill Bradley and Earl Monroe.

And now, today, players such as Bill Cartwright, Bernard King and Truck Robinson. They've taken their places among New York's finest.

NEW LEAGUE, NEW TEAM IN NEW YORK

Few could have suspected what was to come about on June 6, 1946. That's when sports promoters from eleven cities got together and decided to form a professional basketball league.

The new league was called the Basketball Association of America. Its eleven teams were the Boston Celtics, Chicago

The Pearl in action: Earl Monroe outdazzles Celtic Jef Judkins in fourth-period fireworks at Boston Garden. (1979)

Stags, Cleveland Rebels, Detroit Falcons, New York Knickerbockers, Pittsburgh Ironmen, Providence Steamrollers, Toronto Huskies, Washington Capitals, St. Louis Bombers and Philadelphia Warriors.

Three years later, the rival National Basketball League crumbled. Its remaining teams joined the BAA. The league was renamed the National Basketball Association.

The Knicks had an advantage right from the start. Madison Square Garden, which owned the club, put a very special man in charge of the team. His name was Ned Irish. He helped make the Knicks the respected team they are today.

Irish knew basketball and knew basketball fans. Many gave him credit for making college basketball so popular. Irish also knew that to build a first-class organization, you had to treat the players and coaches and fans with class. He did. For example, he gave the team the league's first training camp. The Knicks had the NBA's first athletic trainer. They knew someone cared. And the Knicks were on their way.

Colleges played another big role in the Knicks' development. Most cities have one or two colleges nearby. But New York City had dozens. Some were among the best in the country. Pro teams in the 1940s didn't look all over the country for their

The great Bill Bradley: The sportswriters called him "Mr. Knickerbocker" for his single-minded devotion to the New York team.

players. They signed the best local talent. In New York, the Knicks found plenty.

So the Knicks finished a respectable third place in their Eastern Division in their first BAA season. They won 33 of their 60 games. In the playoffs, New York beat Cleveland twice to advance to the next round. There they collided with the Philadelphia Warriors. The Warriors easily ended the Knicks season. Philly went on to win the first league championship.

Things only got better for the Knicks. Irish robbed the college ranks of one of its best coaches, Joe Lapchick of St. John's University in New York. Lapchick had the best reputation of any coach in New York. His teams had won 181 games and lost just 53.

Though Irish had tried to get Lapchick to join the Knicks in their first season, Lapchick wanted to live up to his contract at St. John's. But as soon as Lapchick was available, Irish was there. The Knicks took another big step toward the top.

SO CLOSE...

Lapchick didn't take long to start molding his new Knicks team.

Dave drives: Number 22 — Dave Debusschere — leaves Baltimore's Wesley Unseld frozen in his tracks in this 1972 aerial display at Madison Square Garden.

One of the first players he added was a 6-foot-5, thin but strong 20-year-old. His name was Carl Braun. Braun already had signed a pro baseball contract to play for a New York Yankees farm club. But Lapchick lured Braun to the Knicks.

Braun was a swingman — he could play either guard or forward. His specialty was a one-handed push shot. Braun took only seven games to figure out how to play in this new league. In one game, he made long shots, short shots, even all eleven of his free-throw attempts. When the final buzzer sounded, Carl Braun had scored 47 points. The rookie had set a new old league scoring record!

Braun played 12 of his 13 seasons in the pros with the Knicks. He was named to the league All-Star game five times. He finished with a New York career average of 14.1 points. He was the Knicks' first superstar.

Harry Gallatin soon followed in Braun's footsteps. The muscular center-forward hailed from Northwest Missouri State. The Knicks picked him first in the 1948 draft. He wouldn't let them down.

Gallatin stood 6-6 and weighed 210 pounds. He was nicknamed "The Horse." Not "The Gazelle" or "The Panther," but "The Horse." Gallatin wouldn't throw any fancy moves at his

Up and over: Marvin Webster (40) rallied from a slump to ignite the Knicks through the "dog days" of the 1983 season.

opponents. But he was so strong, so determined, that he usually got his way.

Lapchick worked Gallatin slowly into New York's starting lineup. But once he got there, "The Horse" wouldn't give up his spot. He played in 682 straight games for the Knicks.

Playing alongside Gallatin and Braun were a few other special players. The 1949 draft brought Vince Boryla, Dick McGuire and Ernie Vandeweghe to the team.

Boryla's hook shot was as trustworthy as a Boy Scout. The Knicks learned that when the game was close and time was running out, Boryla usually could get that hook shot to fall.

McGuire was the Knicks' floor general. All those shooters needed someone to get them the ball. McGuire was their man. In his rookie season, he set a league record for assists. He is second and Braun is third on New York's list for career assists.

Vandeweghe was easy to spot at many Knick practices: He was the one who arrived wearing a white coat and stethoscope. You see, Vandeweghe went to medical school while he was playing for the Knicks. He retired from pro basketball to pursue his medical career. But when he played, Vandeweghe was an all-around offensive threat and menacing defender.

These players slowly raised the quality of the Knicks team. Soon, New York began to make its presence felt in post-season

Haywood goes it alone: Veteran Spencer Haywood finds himself surrounded by Braves in a 1977 match-up in Buffalo.

Pioneers: Wiry Max Zaslofsky (5) of the early Knicks is fouled by Ed Mikan (18) of the Rochester Royals in this 1951 contest at Rochester.

playoffs. The Knicks won the 1949 and 1950 Eastern Division semifinals. But they lost each year in the finals.

Then came 1951. New York edged Syracuse 83-81 in the final game of the Eastern Division series. The Knicks earned their first National Basketball Association division Championship!

The other division champion, the Rochester Royals, wasted little time putting the Knicks into a huge hole in the best-of-seven series. The Royals won the first three games, by an average margin of more than 14 points.

But New York would not give up. That quality would soon become a Knicks trademark. They won Game 4 and then Game 5, in Rochester, where the Knicks hadn't won in three years. Vandeweghe stepped in for Game 6, and led his team to an 80-73 win. The series was tied at three games each. But the Royals finally broke loose enough in the deciding game. Rochester came away with a 79-75 victory and the NBA title.

Remember, now, what happened in the 1950-51 season. The Knicks did almost exactly the same thing in 1952. Most of the core New York players stayed the same: McGuire, Vandeweghe, Gallatin, along with Sweetwater Clifton, Ray Lumpp, Connie Simmons and Max Zaslofsky. But Boryla hurt a knee during the regular season. He had to have surgery and missed the playoffs. Braun served military duty and missed the entire season.

Again, New York beat Syracuse for the division title. This time the championship opponent was Minneapolis. The Lakers featured the league's first dominating big man, 6-10, 245-pound George Mikan. The series see-sawed. New York won Games 2, 4 and 6. Minneapolis won Games 1, 3, 5. The Lakers, unfortunately for the Knicks, stuck to that pattern. They won Game 7 and the NBA crown.

A trend was set, it seemed. The Knicks were a very good team that just couldn't win the big one. New York won a team-record 47 games in 1953. They made it to the finals for the third straight year. But they lost in five games, again to the Lakers.

The longer season began to take its toll on the aging Knicks. Players 30 or 35 years old could still shine when the league had only 48 regular-season games. That's how many games the Knicks played the year over. But by 1956, the NBA had a 72-game season.

New York made it to the playoffs for four more seasons, in 1954, 1955, 1956 and 1957. Then the roof caved in on the House of the Knicks.

Walt Frazier (10) makes a move toward the baseline in a tough clash with the Washington Bullets.

THE DROUGHT

It's the sort of bad spell that creates nightmares.

Starting with the 1957 season, the Knicks finished last ten out of eleven times. All teams get injuries. All teams have stars who eventually retire. Dynasties grow when teams replace their good players with other good players. The Knicks didn't do this during the drought.

Some of the Knicks draft choices were just plain bad. They chose little-known players who never showed much promise for pro basketball. But many other New York picks were simply bad luck. The Knicks would select the obvious top college stars. But often New York would wind up with players who never could adjust to the NBA.

Not all the New York draft picks were flops, of course.

Richie Guerin was a second-round selection in 1954. He didn't get to join the Knicks until the 1956 season because he was drafted into the army. But once he put on his New York uniform, Guerin made his mark. He played eight seasons and averaged more than 20 points per game for the Knicks.

Willie Naulls was a rookie in the 1957 season. He averaged 19.3 points per game in seven seasons with New York.

The great Eddie Miles: In the early 70's, old Number 42 was a force to be reckoned with.

WHAT IS COURAGE? To many New York Knicks fans, courage is Willis Reed playing with a painful hip injury in the 1970 championship series. But an even better example is another Knicks player, Dave Stallworth. On March 7, 1967, Stallworth suffered a heart attack during a New York game with San Francisco. They said he'd never play again. But Stallworth wouldn't give up his dream of returning to the NBA. Hard work and a ton of courage brought Stallworth back for the 1969-70 season. During that championship series against Los Angeles, Stallworth played a key defensive role against Wilt Chamberlain.

The biggest hole was in the middle of the Knicks lineup. They couldn't find a good big man. New York tried center after center, with no luck. The Knicks knew that every great NBA team had a great NBA center. But no one could fill those big shoes in New York.

THE SEEDS ARE PLANTED

At first, New York's 1964 draft looked like the rest of the recent Knicks drafts—nothing special. Their first pick, of course, was a center: Jim Barnes. In the third round, New York took Howard Komives. Later, they picked up Brian Generalovich and Tony Gennari.

Barnes played well in his only season with the Knicks. He averaged 15.5 points per game. Komives tossed in nearly 12 points per season for five years. Generalovich and Gennari didn't make the team.

Oh, what about New York's second-round draft choice in 1964? He was from Grambling University, a small college in the South. But he was a center. The Knicks got lucky. He was still available when their turn came.

A Knick in time: Dick Van Arsdale picks up two against fleet-footed Lenny Wilkens of the St. Louis Hawks. (1966)

"THE NEW YORK KNICKS PICK WILLIS REED."

A love story between a city and a player had just begun.

Pick one word to describe Willis Reed? It would have to be pride. Everything good that came from Reed during his 10 years with the Knicks grew out of that pride.

Reed was insulted that he was only a second-round draft choice. So he proved that he was a first-team NBA All-Star.

Reed's pride was dented when an opposing center would outscore or outrebound him and the Knicks would lose. The next time those two teams met, the other center would have to watch out.

Most of all, Reed's pride carried him and his team through the roughest of times. Behind by 20 or 30 points? Think of your pride and catch up. Down by three points with 10 seconds to go? Have pride, and try your best. Injured and unable to give 100% in a big game? Where's your pride? Go out and do what you can.

Willis Reed did just that. He stood 6-10. More importantly, he carried 240 pounds. No one shoved Willis around. And Reed didn't shy away from a little bit of contact inside.

Reed averaged 19 points and 13 rebounds per game during his 10 years with the Knicks. He never played for another pro team. He played in seven All-Star games. He shined his brightest in the playoffs, when titles and pride were on the line.

Reed battles Hayes: Willis Reed (19) gets off a shot against Elvin Hayes in the first period of a heart-stopper between the Knicks and the Capital Bullets in 1973.

So Reed joined the Knicks in 1964. The next year's draft included Bill Bradley. Cazzie Russell came in 1966. Walt Frazier was the team's top pick in 1967. When the draft jinx ended, so did New York's long drought.

The Knicks made it to the playoffs in 1967 and 1968. But both times they lost in the division semifinals. In 1969, New York made it as far as the division finals before losing to the mighty Boston Celtics. And in 1970, the magic returned to the Big Apple.

THE MAGIC POTION

Reed anchored the middle of the team. The rest of the players concentrated on their own jobs. That combination worked.

In a way, Cazzie Russell was like Ernie Vandeweghe. His love for the game made him a joy to watch. But unlike Vandeweghe, Russell could become an offensive machine. His fall-away jumper could turn into an automatic two points. Best of all, Russell could perform his scoring miracles within seconds of coming off the New York bench. A certain starter for most teams, Russell became one of the Knicks' most valuable substitutes.

Walt Frazier goes high in the air inside two Celtics players for an offensive rebound and an easy two points.

Walt Frazier packed about as much basketball ability into his 6-foot-4 frame as a man could handle. Simply put, Frazier could do it all. He could shoot. He could dribble. He could pass. He could play some of the best defense a team had ever seen. His hands were so quick that sometimes a dribbler wouldn't even know Frazier had knocked the ball away. Already Frazier was speeding away for an easy two points.

Bradley didn't make it to the New York roster until the 1968 season. He had been a superstar with his school books as well as with a basketball at Princeton. He thought his education was more important than his basketball. After he graduated, Bradley was offered a prestigious Rhodes Scholarship to attend school at Oxford University in England. When he finished there, he joined the Knicks.

And in 1969, Dave DeBusschere joined the Kicks in a trade with Detroit. He was the ideal forward: a scorer, rebounder, strong force inside and intimidating defensive player.

Neither Frazier nor Bradley set the league on fire in their first few games. The pressure on them was enormous. Their play showed that. Only William "Red" Holzman could get them relaxed. Red had become New York's coach in the middle of the 1969 season.

Holzman didn't want to coach the Knicks. He was happy as chief of scouting for the team. But he knew the team needed

Bradley's last hurrah: Bill Bradley scores a layup in his final home game with the Knicks in 1977.

FILLING BIG SHOES: When Knicks center Bill Cartwright enrolled at the University of San Francisco, he had some big shoes to fill. Years before, Bill Russell played center for the Dons before moving on to the Boston Celtics and 13 NBA championship seasons. But Cartwright held his own against Russell's shadow. When he left USF, he was both the team's and the league's leading scorer.

help. The Knicks officials thought Holzman could give it to them.

Holzman didn't quite fit in with the New York image. He was rather quiet, not at all flashy or wise-cracking. But he did have firm ideas about how to run a basketball team.

At Holzman's first team meeting, several players showed up a few minutes late. They were fined.

Then Holzman revealed his plan to the Knicks players. They would practice every single day during the season. No days off.

And they would learn how to play defense.

This was no ordinary defense Holzman would have his team play. It was a pressing, swarming, ball-hawking defense.

Best of all, this special defense could work only if the entire team participated. From the high-scoring starters to the substitutes who played only a few minutes each game, each man had to give everything he had.

Holzman took a handful of superb players. He mixed in several other very good ones. And he came out with a team that would give New Yorkers what they had been waiting for since 1947.

KINGS AT LAST

When the Knicks lost to Boston to end their 1969 season, they had just one thing in mind: "Let's win the league title in 1970."

Westphal on a tear: Knicks guard Paul Westphal flies down court as Chicago Bulls' Dave Corzine stretches in vain to block the shot. (1983)

OH, THOSE MCGUIRE BROTHERS! Dick McGuire may have achieved more fame than his brother Al when both played for the New York Knicks. That's probably because Dick was more of an offensive and passing specialist. Al was a defensive whiz. Both went on to become prominent coaches. But now Al has the edge as a celebrity. He left Marquette University to become a college basketball color commentator for television. Dick McGuire went with the Knicks — as the club's chief scout.

Sometimes it's hard to remember how close you came to the championship. It's hard to work for hours every day all summer, practicing your moves. It's hard to remember the big goal when the coach makes the team run lap after lap around the court in practice.

But the Knicks had good memories.

New York won the first five games of the 1969-70 season. Then the lowly San Francisco Warriors handed New York a 112-109 loss. The loss might have been no big deal to most teams. But the Knicks took the loss hard. In the locker room after the game, Reed was almost in tears. That showed how much this season meant to the players.

You might say that the Knicks took that loss to heart. They got a little more determined. Determined enough to win their next 18 straight games! That set a league record for consecutive victories. The Knicks won those 18 games by a huge average of 15 points per game.

The 18th win, the record-setter, showed what New York could do. The Knicks trailed Cincinnati 105-100 with just 27 seconds showing on the clock.

Then, Reed took over in the middle. He asked for a pass inside. He got the ball and was fouled. Unlike some centers, Reed had a super-soft outside shooting touch. He made both free throws. Cincinnati led by three, 105-102.

Slips through Celtics: Willis Reed finds a channel to the hoop in the seventh game of the NBA East playoffs at Boston Garden. (1973)

DeBusschere stole an inbounds pass and scored on a break-away lay-up. 105-104.

Reed batted the ball away from a Royals player, Frazier recovered and, with time running out, shot. It missed. He got his own rebound, and missed again. But this time a Cincinnati player had fouled him. Two seconds showed on the clock when Frazier sank both foul shots. New York won, 106-105

The Knicks lost their next game. The streak was stopped at 18, but their reputation lived on. Now, every team in the league was out to beat them. But that just made the Knicks more determined. New York finished the regular season with 60 wins and just 22 losses.

In the first round of the playoffs, Baltimore fell behind two games to none against New York, then stormed back and won three of the next four to force the seventh game. But pride was on the line. Guess who won? Yep, the Knicks, 127-114.

New York moved on to play Milwaukee in the Eastern Conference finals.

The Bucks boasted a 7-2 rookie center. His name was Lew Alcindor. He later changed his name to Kareem Abdul-Jabbar and became one of the game's all-time superstars. But Alcindor didn't have enough help from his teammates. Reed and his Knicks rolled past Milwaukee in five games.

Strong-armed again: It was big Dave DeBusschere grabbing another rebound against his arch-rivals, the Boston Celtics, in 1974.

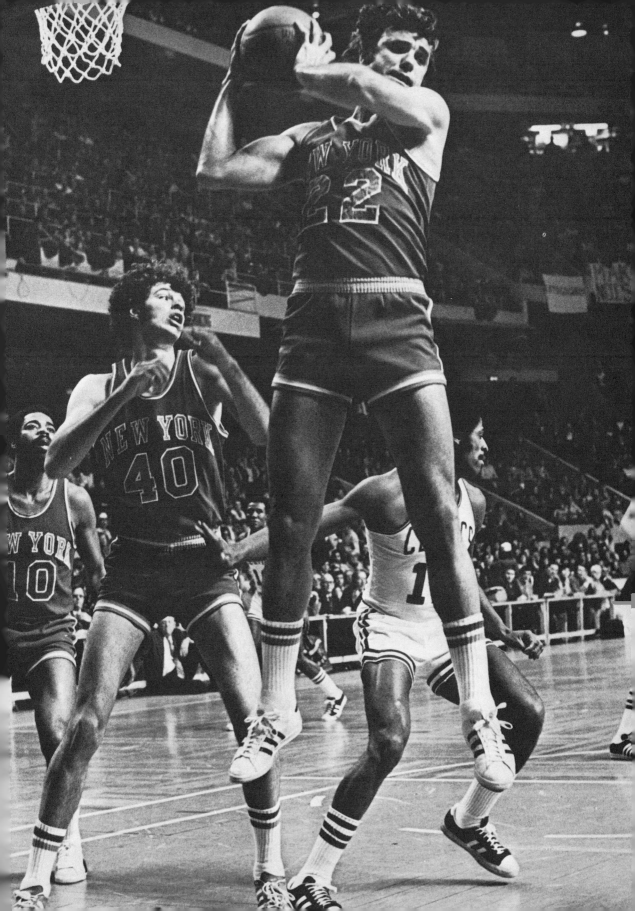

The 1970 championship series was another matter altogether. The Los Angeles Lakers had three of the game's all-time great players: Wilt Chamberlain, Jerry West and Elgin Baylor.

Chamberlin was recovering from an early-season knee injury and surgery. He was barely noticeable in Game 1. The Knicks won, 124-112.

But Wilt had a little pride of his own. He came storming back in Game 2. The Lakers won, 105-103.

Game 3 went down in basketball history, but not because of the final score. The Lakers' Jerry West made a 60-foot shot at the buzzer to send the game into overtime. New Yorkers, however, do remember the final score. New York won in that overtime period, 111-108.

West returned in Game 4 to score 37 points and dish out 18 assists. Los Angeles won, 121-115. The series was tied at two games each.

Game 5 was the turning point of the series, but it turned in a way that wasn't obvious at first.

The first quarter was winding down. The Lakers had taken a big lead over the Knicks. Then, on a drive to the basket, Reed slipped to the floor. He didn't get up. He couldn't. He had pulled a muscle in his hip. Already the big center had been hobbled by aching knees. Now this. The Knicks could almost see their title hopes limp to the locker room along with Reed.

28 points: That's what Campy Russell (number 28) ran up against the Pistons in this action-packed 149-118 victory over the Pistons. (1980)

But that great Willis Reed pride had worn off on a few other players. They thought to themselves, "We can still do it." And you know what? They did.

Holzman rotated his players in and out of the game to keep them fresh. He kept switching New York's defenses to confuse Los Angeles and frustrate Chamberlain. Russell found his shooting groove. Bradley suggested an offense that would give the Knicks' shooters plenty of room. By game's end, the Knicks were back on top, 107-100.

The Lakers came right back to win Game 6 handily, 135-113. But Reed didn't play. Both teams really were gearing up for Game 7 in New York. As the fans and the media crowded into Madison Square Garden, all eyes were on the recovering Willis Reed.

During the pregame warmup, Reed gingerly moved onto the floor. He began shooting some easy free throws. Being careful not to put too much stress on his sore leg, he gently lofted shot after shot through the net. After ten minutes of practice, he limped back to the locker room for more treatment.

Game time approached. Fans worried more as tip-off grew near and Reed still didn't emerge from the locker room. Finally the big guy eased onto the floor for a few more warm-up shots. The ovation from the New York fans was as big as if the championship had been won. Perhaps it had.

Cazzie and Knicks agree: Cazzie Russell, the All-America from the University of Michigan and 1965 Player of the Year, holds the ball in front of Madison Square Garden on the day he joined the Knicks.

41

At the tip-off, Reed didn't even jump against Chamberlain. The Lakers controlled the ball and missed their first shot. Reed limped to the Knicks' offensive end of the court, dragging his nearly useless right leg behind him.

Reed set up at the foul line and waited for a pass. When he received the ball, he faced the basket, looking to pass. Then he bent slightly and launched New York's first shot. It was good! Then, almost unbelievably, Reed scored the Knicks' next basket, too.

As it turned out, those were his only four points of the night. They were enough.

Frazier, DeBusschere and Bradley went to work. Inspired by Reed, they used every bit of their talents. They very nearly blew the Lakers right off the court. By halftime, New York led 61-37. The final score was 113-99.

Many people still believe that, once Reed made his first courageous efforts to play, that score was meaningless. The Knicks would win. They would be the 1970 world champions. And they were.

ONE MORE TIME

Usually the glow of such a championship lasts for years. In many cities, it has, too. World championships don't come easy.

Earl spoils Kupchak's drive: High-flying Mitch Kupchak gets a last-second surprise from Earl "The Pearl" Monroe in 1978 contest at the Garden.

But New Yorkers were treated to two more conference titles and another championship in the next three years.

In 1971, Baltimore's Bullets got their revenge. They took a seven-game series from New York for the Eastern Conference crown.

In 1972, the Knicks beat Boston for that title. Again they met the Lakers for the NBA championship. And again revenge came out on top: The Lakers beat the Knicks, four games to one.

By 1973, the New York roster had changed a little. Earl "The Pearl" Monroe started in the backcourt with Frazier. Jerry Lucas spelled Reed at center, and could also play forward. Henry Bibby and Dean Meminger came off the bench at guard.

Some things remained the same, however. The Knicks won 57 games. They played, and beat, Boston in the Eastern Conference series. They again played Los Angeles in a five-game championship series.

Los Angeles won the first game. Then New York did the impossible. They won the next four games. The Knicks were world champions for the second time in four years!

The Knicks of the past 10 years have been somewhat like those early Knicks teams. On any given night, they could play with the best in the league. But that special balance to win it all wasn't quite there.

Mr. Bibby: Easy-going Henry Bibby was all-smiles until the whistle blew. Here he takes a rare breather at Monmouth College training camp. (1973)

A lot of that has to do with New York's competition. The Atlantic Division of the NBA's Eastern Conference is one of the league's toughest, especially considering the strength of Boston and Philadelphia.

But the Knicks still have been around at playoff time. They took Boston to five games in the Eastern Conference final in 1974. New York also made post-season play in 1975, 1978 and 1981.

Willis Reed tried his hand at coaching for two seasons, 1978 and 1979, but Holzman returned again until Hubie Brown took over as coach for the 1982-83 season.

Brown got the Knicks on his track by the middle of the '83 season. Immediately he gave New Yorkers something to talk about. At one point, the Knicks won 23 of 28 games!

Today, the Knicks' roster just may have those special ingredients that New York came to love in the late 1960s and early 1970s.

No one can tell for sure when the next NBA championship pennant can be hung in New York's Madison Square Garden. But one thing is for sure: Waiting, hoping, the Knicks fans will be there all along the way. Because basketball is their No. 1 game, and the New York Knicks is their No. 1 team.

Smith dodging: Swift-footed Jerry Lucas looks for a way to shoot the gap between the Buffalo Braves' two Smiths — Randy, No. 9, and Elmore, No. 3. (1972)

Action, Knicks-style!